English as she is Fraught

English as she is Fraught

Jonathan Thomas

Illustrated by Graham Allen

Wolfe

First published 1976 by Wolfe Publishing Ltd
10 Earlham Street, London WC2H 9LP

ISBN 0 7234 0706 1

Set by Composing Operations Ltd
Tonbridge, Kent

Printed in Great Britain by
Ebenezer Baylis & Son Limited, The Trinity Press
Worcester, and London

Contents

Introduction and explanation

When Great Britain had a great Empire it held together by the inability of foreigners to understand precisely how it was done.

It depended on the growth of the English Language as the tool of trade and learning and by the simple premise that only an Englishman can understand what he means, because the words he uses are capable of double and triple meanings, most of them dirty.

Failure to understand colloquial usages brought about the expression 'dirty foreigner', because foreigners were always being dirty without realising it. When they weren't being very dirty they were offending people by misusing words without any such intention.

Constantly being in the wrong is character forming and teaches true subservience. Which is how Great Britain got an Empire. Now with the growth of English language teaching through the world, the Empire is shrinking because foreigners are learning how to be rude only when they mean to be rude.

This book is in three parts. The first attempts to guide an overseas visitor into understanding at least something of what is meant when something totally different is said. This part assumes he is here on business – a holidaymaker is not really trying to understand the English for a future relationship, he only wants to enjoy himself.

There is a world of difference, as we shall see, in a couple of words. 'You must come to tea some time', is very different in meaning from 'You must come to tea on Tuesday'.

The second part of the book is a guide through but a few of the minefields. Years of study in some exotic colonial academy like Harvard or Yale will have been wasted if your *faux pas* at your first social gathering are so great that you are never invited again.

"...YOUR DAUGHTER WAS JUST SHOWING ME HER PUSSY WHILE I WAS HAVING MY OATS..."

In a few well thought out grammatically pure sentences it would be possible innocently to suggest that your host is a queer, his daughter of easy virtue and that he is a swindler.

'Good morning sir, I must say you look very gay today. Your daughter was just showing me her pussy while I was having my oats. I also wanted to tell you how much I envy your prowess at fiddling.'

The third part is a collection of short definitions of words with other meanings, similar words likely to cause bother and odds and ends of ambiguity.

What any reader must realise is that you need a really dirty mind to savour all the nuances of our language, otherwise you will not be able to enjoy the clangers of others.

The true aim of this little volume is however much more subtle. After reading it will any foreigner dare to open his mouth? Or will he speak so slowly and in such a considered manner that he will never get a chance to enter a conversation? This will help adjust the present unfortunate strength of the rest of the world and permit the English to start an Empire again.

I've always fancied myself in a pith helmet.

Part one

Understand what is meant

A short guide to guessing what he really means when he says something.

Being met

I'll meet you at the airport
- You are very important

I'll send a car to meet you at the airport
- You are quite important

I'll meet you at the bus town terminal
- Business is terrible and I cannot afford a taxi

I'll expect you at our office in the morning
- I suppose I'll have to face seeing you eventually

Background

What did you study at college?
- I am immature enough to want you to ask about *my* studies, they were at a very smart place

Bargaining

Your price is freight inclusive of course?
- With luck I might persuade you this is normal

Of course the pound won't be devalued
- There's one born every minute

Bribes

It must be nice to be able to afford holidays like that
- I can be bribed

Would you like to join us on our yacht on the Med?
– Can you be bribed?

Business excuses
Cash is a tiny bit tight at the moment
– We're broke
I'm afraid your work doesn't quite suit our present professional needs
– Why bother us with your crazy rubbish?
Our position is slightly strained
– We're broke

Business openers
I know your chairman awfully well
– I once played golf with the old bastard

Civilities
How do you spell your name?
– I've forgotten your name

Credit
We usually request an irrevocable letter of credit and a bank guarantee
– How can you expect to be trusted with a haircut like that?

Deliveries
Yes, we will deliver in two months
– Yes, we will deliver sometime after the strike

Entertaining
Would you like Mr – to show you our beautiful local art gallery?

– I do wish you would push off for a few hours
We are in the middle of the strip club area, I have always wondered what they are like
– I would love you to suggest we visit one
Would you like to see our museums or some London night life?
– I do hope you say night life
Tell your wife we won't be wearing anything fancy
– My wife will be wearing her most expensive outfit
What would you like to drink, we have most things?
– We have whisky, gin and sherry but probably not the foreign muck you want

Family
My daughter is a well built girl
– She is absolutely vast
My daughter is very domesticated
– She is bloody ugly
My wife is a keen golfer and bridge player
– She looks like a horse
My son is not very academic
– He is an idiot

House games
The bathroom is down the hall
– Please don't pee out of the window
Breakfast is at 8 sharp
– By one minute past there will be none left
Breakfast is around 8
– We shall be eating for hours
If you need anything just shout
– Don't you dare

Accepting hospitality
I'll just have a drop
– Fill it up you mean bastard
I prefer a soft chair
– I have haemorrhoids

"MY DAUGHTER IS A WELL BUILT GIRL..."

Invitations to meals and entertaining

You must come and have dinner some time
- Thank goodness you are going, as soon as you have gone I shall tear up your address

Can you come and have dinner on Thursday?
- Can you come and have dinner on Thursday?

Would you and your wife like to come to dinner and a theatre?
- I have an expense account, foreigners are tax deductable and its about time I gave my wife a free evening out

Do stay to tea
- There will be some food

Do have a cup of tea
- That's all you will get

I'll just phone my wife to tell her I'm bringing you for dinner, she will be delighted
- I'll just phone my wife in the hope she won't murder me.

Local events

Grand Church Bazaar
- The neighbourhood's unwanted junk for sale

Grand Gala Opening
- The Mayor (our local tobacconist) will open it wearing a chain of office (and clothes, thank goodness)

Meals

Would you like red or white?
- If you order white with meat I'll never be able to show my face in here again

Would you like a brandy and cigar?
- I am on expenses and would like one myself

Menus

This tastes interesting
- Yugh, lousy foreign muck

I like my meat well done
- Burnt

I like my meat slightly underdone
- Dripping blood

Negotiations
I'll think about it
– No
We'll let you know
– Not bloody likely

Openers
How are you?
– I hope you aren't going to bore me by telling me
How's business?
– I hope you can pay our bill
What are you doing this weekend?
– I think you seem quite a nice chap
Do you ride or shoot or fish?
– Did you have a decent upbringing?
Did you go to a boy's boarding school?
– Are you AC/DC?
It's nice to be away from the family sometimes
– Are you AC/DC?
I have a remote cottage where I like to relax completely at the weekend
– I do hope you are AC/DC
No need to pack anything, come as you are
– Yippee, you are!

Payment
Copy Invoice Please
– I want to delay paying you
We cannot trace your order number
– I want to delay paying you
We paid by airmail bank transfer last week
– We shall pay by surface mail sometime soon

Personal references
His attitude leaves room for improvement
– He is bone idle

He has always handled tasks given him to within the limits of which he is capable
  – He is very stupid
I have never heard anything bad of him
  – I have never heard anything good of him
He is sober, honest and trustworthy
  – He has never been found out

Pleasantries

The toilet is just over there if you want to wash your hands
  – Can't you stop your stomach rumbling?
Do you mind if I open a window?
  – You have farted haven't you?
I wonder if you'd mind awfully waiting outside while I take this phone call?
  – I don't trust you greasy spying foreigners and I want to talk about you
Where are you staying?
  – Can't you do better than that on expenses? I always do
Do have a peppermint, I always suck them
  – Christ! That bloody garlic
May I have your attention please?
  – Shut up
Thank you for dropping in and giving me so much time
  – Why don't you push off, you've been here ages

Position

My husband is a company director
  – My husband could either be director of a vast company or run a one man fish and chip shop with limited liability so he can fiddle expenses

Promotion

These items will be heavily promoted worldwide
  – Some modest advertising is possible if you insist

Protocol
The chairman is rather tied up but has asked his personal assistant to see you
– You are not very important
He has asked the Managing Director to see you
– You are too important to offend

Quality
I expect you will want the de-luxe model
– The ordinary one doesn't work

On the railway
The next train on Platform 5 is for Upshot, Bagshot and Portsmouth
– Check with three people and the next train *may* be the . . .
British Railways regret the delay to your train and its late arrival
– The driver overslept
Is there room for one more?
– Move up fatso

References
Haven't you any London references?
– How can you expect me to trust that foreign rubbish?

Reports
He replied with less than his usual candour
– He is lying again
He suggested a statesmanlike solution
– He has managed to wriggle out of it again

The sack
You don't feel very happy here do you?
– I wish you would push off before I sack you
You have been tired lately, I think you need a change
– I wish you would push off before I sack you

Schools

Are your children away at school?
– Mine are away at expensive posh boarding schools

I believe in State education
– Mine are not away at school

We believe in discipline at this school
– We beat the pupils

We believe in self expression at this school
– We permit experimental sex

Your boy is not very scholarly
– He is as thick as two planks

Secretarial excuses

Mr Brown has just gone to lunch
– He won't be back until 3.30

We tried several times to ring you back
– I hope you believe this twaddle

Mr Brown is so sorry to keep missing you
– He is not trying very hard

I'm sorry, I told him you were waiting
– He's trying to face up to seeing you eventually

Mr Brown is away with a cold
– It's a nice day for golf

Mr Brown's taking sick leave
– He is a civil servant taking all buckshee time he is allowed

Mr Brown is busy dictating
– Mr Brown has a lovely new secretary with big boobs and does not wish to be disturbed

Yes, I did tell him you called and he said he would contact you the minute he could
– Get lost

In the shop

We've just sold the last one of what you wanted
We don't stock rubbish like that

"WE BELIEVE IN SELF-EXPRESSION AT THIS SCHOOL"

Smoking
I don't smoke but please do if you wish
– I hope you won't, it makes me cough

Sociability
Do you live near the lake? Mountain? Sea? Beach? River?
– My ghastly scruffy teenage children may descend on you next summer
Will you accept a transfer charge call from — ?
– Hard luck, they have arrived

Street notices
Babette, new young model
– Babette, elderly prostitute
Cuddly kitten for sale
– Pussy (see p 62) available by the hour
Miss Lasham, discipline classes
– Perverts catered for
Erection construction and demolition
– What goes up must come down

Time
Our office opens at 9.30
– With luck someone will be in by 10
Our warehouse can receive goods up to 5 pm
– Our warehouse manager locks the receiving bay at 3.30
Can you spare me 5 minutes?
– I shall be with you for at least an hour
Mr Brown won't keep you a moment, he's just finishing a conference
– Take your shoes off, you'll be here hours
I'm in the office quite early
– Try after 10
I work quite late
– I'm gone by about six

Travel

Do you have a factory or office in Sweden or Denmark I could visit?

– I would love to see some live sex shows

Visits

I called because you are one of the most important businessmen here

– Your name was the only one in bold type in the directory

The weather

Bright and sunny

– It will probably rain

Misty

– It will probably rain hard

Wet

– Send for Noah

Weekend

You must come down one weekend

– Not if I can help it

You must come down next weekend

– We would love to have you

Work force

We have some slight production difficulties

– The men are on strike

There are some administrative delays

– The men are on strike

Some shipping documents have been misplaced

– The men are on strike

Our quality controllers want another look

– The men are on strike

Our delivery truck broke down

– The men are on strike

Part two

The careful use of words

The following list is not claimed to be a complete guide to possible *double entendre* but should be sufficient to make you realise that English is not a language to be trifled with and that you should never open your mouth unless you really know what you are saying. Not all the words, expression or meanings are parlour level but none are so obscure as to be totally unlikely.

Abusing
He was abusing her
– He was shouting rudenesses at her
He was abusing himself
– He was masturbating

A/C D/C
Is your home A/C or D/C?
– Is the electricity at your house alternating or direct current?
Are you A/C or D/C at home?
– Are you heterosexual or homosexual at home?
Are you A/C and D/C at home?
– Are you bisexual?

Acid
Don't give me the acid
– Do not give me the acidic substances
Don't give me the old acid
– Don't try to fool me with a lot of nonsense
Don't give me any acid
– I'm not fond of LSD

Acres
He gave him several acres
– He presented him with a lot of land
He gave him a pair of achers
– He kicked him where it would hurt the most

Adjusting
He was adjusting his jacket
– He was altering the position of his jacket
He was adjusting his clothing
– He was doing up the front of his trousers

Admit
She openly admitted her guilt
– She fully confessed
She often openly admitted it
– She was frequently willing and able

Adrift
The sailor was adrift
– He was loose in an open boat without oars or sail
The soldier was adrift
– He was a deserter

Adult
I look forward to adult life
– I want to be grown up
I look forward to a life of adultery
– I wish to spend my time having illicit sex relations with the spouses of others

Affair
She was organising a smart affair
– She was a superb hostess
She was having an affair
– She was indulging in a sexual relationship

Aid
She sought aid
– She looked for help
She sought A.I.D.

– She wanted to conceive a child through artificial insemination

Airy fairy
He is a bit airy fairy
– He flits around in discussions without any concrete results
He is a very 'airy fairy
– He is an extremely hirsute homo

Alley
It sounds as if it is up your alley
– It seems to be suitable for your experience
Up your alley
– Is a rather obvious rude remark

Altogether
Shall we come in all together?
– There are a lot of us and we ask if we should all arrive at the same time
Shall we come in the altogether?
– Is it an orgy where we are expected to arrive without any clothing?

Annually
He earned a lot annually
– He received a considerable income each year
He earned a lot anally
– He was either a surgeon specialising in haemorrhoids *or* he hired out his rectum

Apparatus
He showed me the apparatus
– He displayed the equipment for performing the task
He showed me his apparatus
He displayed his personal male equipment for performing the task

Appendix/appendage
He had his appendix out
– He had an internal part at the bottom of his intestines surgically removed

He took the appendix out
– He removed the book's subsidiary additions
He had his appendage out
– He had forgotten to do up the front of his trousers

Arsenic
He gave her arsenic
– He poisoned her with a chemical
He gave her arse a nick
– He cut her nether regions with a sharp object

Athletic
He has athletic feet
– His feet look muscular
He has athlete's foot
– He has a fungal foot disease

Athletics
He looks like an athletics supporter
– He appears to follow athletic meetings
He looks like an athletic supporter
– His face resembles a jock strap designed to contain male whatsits

Bag
I left my old bag in the hotel
– *either* My old suitcase is still at the hotel
or My accommodating but somewhat worn out willing female companion is still at the hotel

Bang
She wore her hair in a bang
– She had an old-fashioned hair style with a bobble of hair at the front
He is inside making a bang
– He is preparing a minor explosion
He is inside having a bang
– He is inside having sexual relations

Basket
What a nice little basket
 – *either* That wicker carrying object is nice
 or What a pleasing illegitimate child

Batter
That baker is mixing the batter
 – He is putting the flour and eggs together
That baker is on the batter
 – He is currently engaged in sexual contortions

Beans
We have no beans
 – We do not have a supply of edible pulses
I haven't a bean
 – I am broke and without any money

Bear
She was so heavy he was not able to bear her over the threshold
 – She was rather fat
She was unbearable
 – Her behaviour was so unpleasant that nobody wanted to meet her

Beat
The policeman is on his beat
 – He is walking around the area allocated to him
That policeman has got a beat
 – He has got an erection

Bend
He is just the other side of the bend
 – He is waiting round the curve
He is round the bend
 – He is a nut without proper mental faculties

Bit
I would like a bit of this
 – I would like a bit of this

I would like a bit of the other
– I fancy some sex relations

I am doing my bit
– *either* I am playing my fully responsible part in the operation
or I am having sex relations with the young woman with whom I consort

Bog

Be careful, there is a bog over there
– Watch how you walk, the ground is marshy

There is a bog over there
– There is a toilet over there

Bogies

– *either* Policemen
or Things supporting railway carriages
or Imaginary frightening creatures
or Mucillous lumps hanging from the nose

(– "The bogies looked like giving way and dropping on the crowd below" – could mean lots of things)

Boob

I made a big boob
– I made a very silly mistake

That maid has big boobs
– That lady servant has large noticeable breasts (See also **Tits**)

Boot

I am going out in my old boots
– I have old footwear with ankle protection on my feet

I am going out with an old boot
- I am consorting with an extremely willing and well used female

He went out with a pair of old boots
– He was wearing ancient heavy footwear
or He went out with a couple of well worn ancient willing females

Buff
I would like you to buff this metal tray
  – Can you polish it with a cloth?
I would like to see you in the buff
  – Get undressed

Bum
He is a fat bum
  – He is a corpulent tramp
He has a fat bum
  – His behind is very large

Bunk
He needs a bunk up
  – He requires assistance in reaching a greater height
She needs a bunk up
  – Suggests she is somewhat on heat

Buns
She has a plate of buns in the oven
  – She is cooking some pastry for us
She has a bun in the oven
  – She is pregnant

Buttering
These sandwiches need buttering
  – This bread should have butter put on it
He needs buttering (up)
  – It is necessary to flatter him and say all sorts of nice things to him

Call of Nature
I hear the call of Nature
  – I can hear the little birds in the trees
I am answering the call of Nature
  – I am having a pee

Camp/camping
Are you camping here?
  – Are those your tents where you are staying?

"SHE NEEDS A BUNK UP..."

Are you camp here?
– Are you a bunch of homosexuals?

Cap
She always wears a cap
– *either* She prefers a flat cloth hat
or Her contraceptive method is a dutch cap

Carve
The meat is being carved up
– It is being sliced
We are being carved up
– We are being cheated

Chair
He took a chair
– He sat down
He took the chair
– He sat down as chairman of the meeting
He got the chair
– He was killed by the electric chair

Chamber
He is seated in the chamber
– He is in a small room
He is seated on the chamber
– He is sitting on a po

Chaps
He has chaps
– *either* He suffers from dry rough skin
or He owns leather riding trousers
or He has sex with males

Chaste/chased
She loves being chaste
– She revels in her purity
She loves being chased
– She likes men after her

Cheap skate
He is always known for his cheap skate
– He is a fishmonger who sells skate cheaply
He is always known as a cheap skate
– He is a cheating, penny pinching, corner cutting type

Cheeks
He saw her rosy cheeks
– *either* She displayed the reddish sides of her face
or She displayed the reddish sides of her buttocks

Cheeses
Smelly cheeses are sold at a grocery shop or delicatessen
Smelly cheesers are noticed among those who should change their socks or wash their feet more often

Cherry
She gave him a cherry
– She gave him a fruit
She gave him her cherry
– She let him take her virginity

Chips
He ate his chips
– He ate his French fried potatoes
He had his chips
– He got killed or something terrible happened to him

Chisel
He is good at chiselling
– He does well chipping away slivers of wood with a sharp metal tool
He is a good chiseller
– He is good at cheating people

Chop
He went to the butchers and got a chop
– He got a piece of bony rib meat
He got the chop
– He was sacked

Chopper
He charged at her with his chopper
– *either* He rushed towards her waving a metal implement
or He rushed towards her with his favourite fleshy implement

Circum-
He was completely circumscribed
– He was bound in by numerous rules and obligations
He was circumspect
– He was very cautious and wary
He was completely circumcised
– The foreskin of his penis had been completely removed

Clapped
He was often clapped out
– He was frequently exhausted
He got clapped very often
– He got applause frequently
He got clap very often
– He got gonorrhoea often
He has a clapped out old banger
– He has an old broken down noisy car
She is a clapped out old banger
– She is a diseased old promiscuous female

Cleaners
I am going to the cleaners
– My suit needs cleaning
I am being taken to the cleaners
– I am being cheated

Club
My wife joins clubs
– She joins associations
My wife is in the club
– She is pregnant

Cock
He talked a lot of cock
– He spoke rubbish

He fixed a ball cock
  – He did some plumbing and mended a valve in the cistern
He made a total cock up
  – He made a complete mess
He had a total cock up
  – He got in a long way
That farmer has a hell of a lot of big cocks
  – He has very many male chickens
That farmer has one hell of a big cock
  – His trousers bulge incredibly

Cod

Go down to the fishmonger for a piece of cod
  – Fetch me a piece of fish
Go to the theatrical costumiers for a cod piece
  – I want an item as worn in regency times to increase the bulge in a man's trousers

Coil

She is in the other room fitting a coil
  – *either* She is keen on making radios and is assembling a vital part
  or She is keen on contraception and is fitting an intra-uterine device to her vital parts

Commode

I am sorry to incommode you
  – I am sorry to cause inconvenience
I am sorry you are stuck in the commode
  – Your bottom is stuck in a chamber pot placed in a chair

Conception

The scientist had no conception of the size of his task
  – He did not appreciate how great was the requirement
Conception took place later
  – At home in bed he implanted his wife with a seed she fertilised

Conjugation, etc.
He always got his conjugations right
– His grammar was impeccable
He always got his conjugal rights
– His wife had to be able, ready and willing whenever he wanted

Consummate
She was a consummate artist
– She was brilliant as a painter
She was a consummated artist
– Her husband did a good job on her

Continent
He is on the continent
– He is visiting Europe's mainland
He is incontinent
– He pees himself

Copper
Give me a copper
– Let me have a small amount of money
Fetch me a copper
– Get me a policeman

Correspondence
I got a letter in French yesterday
– I correspond with a French national
I got a French letter yesterday
– I found somewhere where male contraceptives are sold in ones instead of threes

Correspondent
He is a frequent correspondent
– He writes many letters
He is a frequent co-respondent
– He has been cited as the other man in many divorce cases

Corporation
The chairman had a big corporation
– *either* His company group was large

or He had a great fat belly

Crabs

He caught crabs at the seaside

– *either* He trapped shellfish at the seaside

or He caught sexually transmitted subcutaneal parasites while on a dirty weekend at the coast

Craft

A craftsman takes pride in his manual skills

An arty crafty person makes delicate fancy bits and pieces

A crafty person is low and cunning sorting things for his own benefit

Craps

Come round for some craps

– Let us play with dice

Don't talk such crap

– Don't talk nonsense

Do have a crap

– Do go to the toilet to relieve your burden

The creek

The boat is up the creek

– The vessel is in a narrow side part of the river

We are up the creek

– We are in terrible trouble without obvious means of propelling ourselves out since such ordure would require a strong paddle and we do not have one

Crutch/crotch

She was leaning on her crutch

– The poor one legged lady was leaning on a wooden support apparatus

She was leaning on his crotch

– She was leaning on the fork of his trousers where it would hurt the most

Cut

He is very deeply cut

– He has a gaping wound

"THE CHAIRMAN HAS A BIG CORPORATION"

He is well and truly cut
  – He is extremely drunk

Defect, etc.
The Russian defected to the West
  – He left his party to come to England
The Russian defecated to the West
  – He did his stools in a westerly direction

Dewdrop
Look at those glorious drops of dew
  – The grass is glistening in the morning light
Look at those dewdrops
  – Those horrible bits dangling from their noses

Dick
She was crazy for Dick
  – She was madly in love with Richard
She was crazy for dick
  – She was constantly in need of sex

Dicky
I am feeling dicky
  – I don't feel well
I am feeling my dicky
  – I am indulging in onanism

Dike
That looks like a dike
  – *either* That looks like a drainage ditch or embankment
  or That looks like a lesbian

Dip
He popped in for a quick dip
  – *either* The swimming pool was near and he had a short swim
  or His willing girl friend was near and he had a short sexual gratification

Doodah

I feel all of a doodah

– I am nervously excited

I feel all of your doodah

– I have my hand completely covering your private parts

The door

She showed him to the door

– She politely escorted him to the door as a parting gesture

She showed him the door

– She threw him out

Dose

Has she taken a dose?

– Has she imbibed her medicine in the required quantity?

Has she got a dose?

– Is she suffering from an unfortunate social disease?

Drag

He is an awful drag

– He is very boring

He is awful in drag

– He is not attractive when dressed in female clothing

Draw

She showed me the contents of her drawer

– She went through the papers and things in the section of her desk

She showed me the contents of her drawers

– She displayed what was in her knickers

Dress

My husband always dresses on the left

– *either* His wardrobe is on the left of the bedroom so he puts his clothes on over there

or He always lets his dingle dangle down his left trouser leg

Duck

I want a duck and a goose

– I wish to purchase two items of poultry

I want a goose and duck
– I need sexually gratifying

Ejaculate
'Good Heavens', he ejaculated
– A sudden burst of phrase came from him
His ejaculation was premature
– His sexual seminal emission could not be kept back

End
He is keeping his end up
– He is behaving with determination and making his presence felt
He is getting his end away
– He is succeeding in obtaining sexual favours

Enemy
Those are the enemies of the people
– They are the foes
Those are the enemas of the people
– They are surgical inserts to permit easier bowel evacuation

Erection
The building is in course of erection
– The building is being built
The builder has an erection
– His thingy has gone all stiff

Excuse
He excused himself
– He politely showed he wanted to leave
He asked to be excused
– *either* He politely requested them to understand he could not be present
or He wanted to go to the toilet

Expose
Let me expose my ideas to you
– I hope to sell you some things by talking about my idea
Let me expose myself to you
– I wish to undress my private parts for you to see

Eyewash

There is the eyewash
 – There is the liquid for washing your eyes
That is eyewash
 – That is untrue rubbish

Face ache

He has a face ache
 – The poor man has neuralgia or dental trouble
He is a face ache
 – His presence is very unpleasant and undesirable

Fags

He felt fagged
 – He was tired out
She gave him some fag ends
 – She made a meal for him from left over oddments
He felt for a fag
 – *either* He reached out for a cigarette
 or He had feelings of brotherhood towards a homosexual

Faggot

He had faggot with his chips
 – He had a chopped meat sausage with his fried potatoes
He had chips with his faggot
 – He had fried potatoes with his homosexual boyfriend

Fanny

I'd like to show you our Fanny
 – Our daughter is called Frances, and Fanny for short
I'd like to show you my fanny
 – I am a lady of easy amusement and desire to display my pudenda

Father

Shall we have some?
 – Let us eat some
How is your father?
 – I do hope your parent is well

Shall we have some how's your father?
  – Let us enjoy some sex

Fellow feeling
I have fellow feeling in my bosom
  – I like humanity and am kind to everyone
I have a fellow feeling in my bosom
  – This man whose name I do not know is playing with my titties

Fiddle
He plays the fiddle
  – He plays the violin
He is on the fiddle
  – He is cheating his employer

Flash
He is a flash dresser
  – He wears loud clothes
He is a flasher
  – In hot weather he enjoys displaying his organ to others

Flies
Just a moment while I undo my flies
  – *either* I am a fisherman and have some imitation fly fishing lures to undo
    or I intend opening the front of my trousers for whatever useful purpose comes to mind
There are flies on me
  – Help remove these insect pests
There are no flies on me
  – I am very bright and not easily fooled

Form
He has good form
  – He is very fit and playing his sport well
He has form
  – He has been to jail

Frigid
She was extremely frigid towards him
- She was cold and unfeeling towards him
She was extremely frigid with him
- She was unable to achieve sexual gratification with him

Fruit
I feel like some fruit
- Those apples look very nice
I feel fruity
- I am in need of sexual relief

Game
He is not playing the game
- He is behaving in an ungentlemanly fashion
I like game
- I like eating wild creatures like partridge or hare
She plays a good game
- She is a fine sportswoman
She is on the game
- She is a professional prostitute

Gay
Used to mean happy and uninhibited. Now it means homosexual – be warned. Thus:
He is a bachelor gay
- He is an unfettered carefree fickle male
He is a gay bachelor
- He is unmarried and prefers sex with men

Gobble
She gobbles her food
- She takes it down at great speed without chewing it properly
She is a gobbler
- She enjoys varieties of oral sex

Good turn
He did her a good turn
- *either* He was kind and helped her with a problem
  or He helped her slight sex starvation problem

Grass/turf

He was warned to keep off the grass
- They didn't want to spoil the new grass seed

He was warned off the turf
- His malpractices meant he was no longer allowed to participate in matters relating to the racing of horses

Grind

It was hard grind
- It was very hard work

She was a hard grind
- Sex relations with her were not easy or pleasant

Gross

What do you gross?
- How much do you make before overheads?

Give me a gross
- Let me have 144

You are very gross
- You are coarse and disgusting

Ha'penny

She had her hand on a ha'penny
- She touched a halfpenny coin

She had her hand on her ha'penny
- She touched her whatsit

Habit

That monk has a dirty habit
- His clerical garb needs washing

Those monks have dirty habits
- They pick their noses or are similarly disgusting

Handful

She was quite a handful to handle
- She was difficult to organise

She let him have a handful
- She enjoyed being fondled intimately

Hanky panky

There is some hanky panky going on here
- Something somewhat dishonest is going on here

Do you fancy some hanky panky?
- Get undressed

Happy look/glad eye

She gave him a happy look
- She smiled pleasantly at him

She gave him the glad eye
- Her glance showed she would fancy amorous advances from him

Head

He has got a large head
- He takes a large size in hats and is probably brainy

He is a big head
- He has an inflated view of his own importance

He is a head
- He takes drugs

He is on the head
- He is sitting on the ship's latrine

High

How high are you?
- What is your height?

Are you high?
- Are you drunk or drugged?

Himself

He played by himself
- He played on his own

He played with himself
- He played with his own

Homely

What a homely room
- Isn't it nice and comfortable

What a homely wife
- God! isn't she ugly

Hot

He is in the hot seat
- He is responsible for everything

She's got a hot seat
- She is constantly in need of sex

She is wearing hot pants
- She is clothed in modern tight fitting short trousers

She has got hot pants
- She is constantly in need of sex

Hot stuff

This is hot stuff
- This tastes like curry

She is hot stuff
- She is a vivacious attractive girl

She is a hot stuff
- She is sexually outstanding

House

She is the lady of the house and called madam
- Her husband owns it and she insists servants address her respectfully

She is the madam of a house
- She runs a brothel

Her house is full
- Every room is taken

She has a full house
- She has a winning poker hand
  or She is suffering from every known venereal disease concurrently

Hum

A bee hums and makes a buzzing noise

He is humming
- He is making a musical noise

He hums
- He is extremely malodorous

Insoluble/insolvent
The trouble is, his product is insoluble
– It will not dissolve
The trouble is, his company is insolvent
– It is bankrupt

Intercourse
He enjoys social intercourse
– He enjoys mixing with people
He enjoys intercourse
– He enjoys sexual gymnastics

Interfere
He interfered with her plans
– He prevented her carrying out her objectives
He interfered with her
– The dirty devil laid hands on her undergarments and private parts

Intimate
She was very intimate with him
– She confided her secrets to him
She was intimate with him
– She confided her body to him

Intolerant/intolerable
He is intolerant
– He does not suffer fools gladly
He is intolerable
– He is a fool and unbearable

Jerk
He is a jerk
– He is a no good nonentity
He jerked himself out of his lethargy
– He pulled himself together and stopped his inaction
He jerked himself
– He masturbated

Job
He is looking for a job
– He is seeking employment
He is doing a job
– He is currently employed at a task
He is on the job
– He is engaged in sex

Jockey
He went out with a short jockey
– He went off with a small man who rides horses for a living
He went out with his jockey shorts
– He went out wearing tight fitting underpants

John
I am going to John
– I am going to see Jonathan
I am going to the John
– I am going to the toilet

Jug
He has been at the jug
– He has been boozing
He has been in the jug
– He has been in prison

Jump
He had his first jump today
– He has just started parachute training
– He has just started sex

Kinky
My boots have a kink in them
– My footwear has a deep crease
I have kinky boots
– I wear thigh length fashion footwear designed to appeal to men's base instincts
The surface is a bit kinky
– It has rucks or kinks in it
He is kinky

– He enjoys exotic and weird sex practices

Knackers
Are *either* People who buy up broken down horses for slaughter and sale
or Testicles

Knee tremble
His knees are trembling
– He is terrified
He is having a knee tremble
– The cad has the girl up against the wall and is having his evil way in an upright position

Knockers
What beautiful fancy knockers
– *either* How pleasing are those elaborate metal fixtures on those doors
or What pleasantly rounded ladies' bosoms

Knock up
They are having a knock up
– *either* They were tennis players practising before a game
or They were in the middle of a totally different game
She was knocked up
– *either* The hotel porter gave her an early call by rapping on the door
or Something else was being used to knock with

Labour
She was canvassing in a Labour ward
– *either* She was seeking votes in a division of a constituency that habitually votes for the Labour Party
or She was seeking support in a hospital ward where ladies were giving birth

Lagging
He got lagging
– He got stuff to put round pipes to stop them freezing
He got a lagging
– He got sent to prison for a long time

Lay

Lays of ancient Rome
- Narrative poems by Lord Macaulay
  or Willing females of the old imperial capital

Leak/leek

I want a leek
- I need a vegetable of the onion family

He has a leak upstairs
- The pipes are bad and he needs a plumber

He had a leak upstairs
- He went upstairs to have a pee

Leery

He was an extremely leery character
- *either* He was sly in everything he did
  or He went round making suggestive facial expressions

Light fingers

He has light fingers
- He is very gentle

He is light fingered
- He is a thief and picker up of unconsidered trifles

Lumber

He went out and got lumber
- He fetched some timber

He went to the lumber room
- He went into the room full of junk, useless and unwanted things

He went out and got lumbered
- He acquired a whole load of tasks and responsibilities he could well have done without

Maidenhead

He played with her at Maidenhead
- He played at a Berkshire town by the River Thames

He played with her maidenhead
- He played with her virginity

Make

He is always making things
  – He enjoys building things with his hands

He is always on the make
  – He is constantly concerned with trying to get a profit from everything

Mark

He marked his card
  – He gave hints and tips and information that would give him an advantage

He marked his cards
  – The low down chap put secret signs on a pack of cards so he could win by cheating

Meal

Enjoy your meal
  – I hope it tastes good

Don't make such a meal out of it
  – Stop going on and on about things

Member

I'd like you to meet our member
  – This is our parliamentary representative

I'd like to show you my member
  – I am a dirty exhibitionist about to display my whatsit

Mince

I like the way my butcher minces
  – *either* The manner in which he chops up meat is pleasing to me
  or The effeminate knees-together wobbly way he walks pleases me

Naked

He showed her his naked weapon
  – *either* He showed his sword was not in its scabbard
  or He displayed his unadorned privates

Naturalist/naturist

He is a naturalist
  – He studies wild life
He is a naturist
  – He goes round naked

Needle

She has got the needle
  – *either* She is about to do some sewing
    or She is extremely annoyed

Nest

He is looking at a bird's nest
  – He is interested in our feathered flying friends
He is on the nest
  – He is having sex

Nibble

He was nibbling at his food
  – He was pecking at it in small bites
He was having a nibble
  – He was enjoying sexual favours

Notice

He gave her a notice
  – He presented her with a sheet containing some information
He gave him notice
  – He sacked him

Nut

Here is a nut
  – Here is the edible vegetable
He is a nut
  – He is pleasantly eccentric
He is a nutter
  – He is mentally unbalanced
Kick him in the nuts
  – Aim your kick at his genitals

Old man

Let me introduce you to my Old Man
- *either* A lady informally introducing you to her husband
  or If you are a young man it could be your father
  or If you are female it could be a low down male wishing to give you a demonstration of his male model

Organ

I would like to play on your organ
- May I try your musical instrument?

'Labour Weekly' is the organ of the Labour Party
- This left wing newspaper is the mouthpiece of the Labour Party

I would like to play with your organ
- Your sex parts fascinate me

Other

I would like a bit of the other one
- May I have some of that alternative dish?

I would like a bit of the other
- I fancy some sex

Overdue

She is now three weeks overdue
- *either* She should have paid three weeks ago
  or Her monthly period is late

Packet

He caught a packet
- *either* Someone threw a small box and he caught it
  or He got on a smallish passenger boat
  or He got varieties of VD

Particulars

A policeman came and took down her particulars
- He wanted details of her name, address and so on

Her boy friend took down her particulars
- He removed her nether garments

"I WOULD LIKE TO PLAY
WITH YOUR ORGAN"

Passage
He blocked her passage
- This man stood in her way and prevented her progress
- This low chap had sexual relations with her

Passed
He passed a stream
- He walked by the side of a small flow of water

He passed water
- He urinated

Penal/penile
Penal strictures are rules laid down to clarify punishment
Penile strictures are excrutiatingly painful and prevent the passing of a man's water

Penny pincher
He is a penny pincher
- He is mean and tight and saves hard

He pinches pennies
- He steals small sums

Perish
He is perished
- He is cold and frozen

He is a perisher
- He is a bit of a so and so

Pets
The young couple are in the pet business
- They run a shop selling animals

The young couple are busy petting
- They are kissing and cuddling and doing everything but that

Piddle
A piddler is one who passes water
One who piddles about is one who plays around at tasks without getting things sorted out

Piles
That pier is on piles
– That structure sticking in the water is placed on large blocks of wood
That peer has piles
– That member of the House of Lords has haemorrhoids
You don't have to offer him money, he has obviously got piles
– *either* He is filthy rich
or He suffers from a painful anal condition

Pips
He gave me the pips
– He gave me the fruit stones
He gave me the pip
– He got on my nerves

Pissed
He was pissed off
– He was very fed up
He pissed off
– He went away
He was very pissed
– He was extremely drunk
He pissed
– He urinated

Pleasure
It was a pleasure to do business with her
– It was pleasing to have a business relationship with her
It was a business to do pleasure with her
– It was hard going to have sex with her

Po
He was very po faced
– He had a stern blank disapproving expression
He had a face like a po
– His features resembled a chamber pot

Poke
He gave her a poke
– He prodded her with his finger

He poked her
  – He prodded her with something else somewhere else

Poof
He disappeared with a poof of smoke
  – The conjurer vanished in a small haze of fumes
He disappeared to the smoke with a poof
  – He vanished to London with a homo

Pooped
I was pooped
  – I was completely worn out
I was pooping
  – I was in the toilet doing solids

Porridge oats
He is having his porridge oats
  – He is breakfasting on coarse meal
He is having his oats
  – He is engaged in sexual dalliance
He is doing porridge
  – He is in prison

Potent
He is a potent advocate for our cause
  – He speaks strongly for us
He is an impotent advocate
  – He cannot produce the necessary for procreation

Pounced/ponced
He pounced on her
  – He leapt upon her like a cat
He ponced on her
  – He lived on her immoral earnings

Prick
He pricked his finger
  – He stuck a sharp point in his finger
He fingered his prick
  – He put his hands on his male whatsit

Privates

The Colonel then showed her his privates

– *either* The commanding officer pointed to his ordinary unranked troops

or He displayed his genitalia

Privy

He is a Privy Counsellor

– He advises the Queen

He is privy to state secrets

– He is trusted with important confidential information

He is in the privy

– He is in the latrine

Probation

He was on probation

– *either* He was being tried out to see if he would succeed at a task

or He had been to court, told he was naughty and given a chance so long as he reported his progress to an officer of the court

Prostitute

She was prostituting her talent

– She was allowing her skills to be wasted in unworthy directions

Her talent was prostitution

– She was great at the world's oldest profession

Pup

He was sold a pup

– *either* The petshop sold him a baby dog

or The article he bought was no good at all

Pussy

Show me your pussy cat

– Let me see your feline furry pet

Show me your pussy

– Let me see your female fur

Queer

You are trying to queer my pitch
– You are trying to disrupt my successful proceedings
You are trying to pitch my queer
– You have my homosexual in your arms and are trying to throw him
I feel queer
– I feel queasy and unwell
I feel a queer
– I handle a homo

Quick one

Come in for a quick one (from a man)
– Let us have a quick drink
Come in for a quick one (from a woman)
– We have five minutes before my husband gets home

R's

She has a fascinating way of rolling her r's
– She has a pleasantly resonant manner of speaking when pronouncing the letter r
She has a fascinating way of rolling her arse
– She has a pleasantly wobbling movement of her buttocks

Randy

I am Randy
– *either* My name is Randolph but I am called Randy by friends
or I am constantly sexually aroused

Raspberry

He gave him some raspberries
– He gave him some small berry fruits
He gave him a raspberry
– He indicated his contempt by making a blubbery noise

Ravishing

She was ravishing
– She was unbelievably beautiful
She was ravished
– She was raped

Relations
They are upstairs having relations to tea
– They are giving a light meal to their relatives
They are having relations upstairs
– They are in bed doing this and that

Revolting
My workmen are revolting
– *either* My staff are about to strike
or My staff have disgusting habits

Riddle
My son has a riddle for you
– My son will ask you a joke question with a feeble funny answer
Our maid is just riddling the grate
– She is shaking out the ashes stuck in it
I just have to have a riddle
– I really must urinate

Ring
She showed him her ring
– *either* She displayed her jewellery
– *or* She displayed her female anatomy

Row
He is having a row
– He is in a boat, rowing
He is having a row
– He is in an argument

Rowlocks
Are things on boats that hold the oars and are pronounced 'rollocks'
'Rollocks' is an expletive meaning testicles

Rubber

Can you lend me a rubber?
 – I want to erase some pencil notes
Can you lend me some rubbers
 – I am sexually very active and have run out of contraceptives

Run

I have got to run
 – I am in a hurry and really must go
I have got the runs
 – I must find a toilet rapidly as my stomach is misbehaving something rotten

Satisfied

I am well satisfied
 – I am extremely pleased
I have been well satisfied
 – I have enjoyed sexual fulfilment

Sauce/saucy

She has got the sauce
 – She has been to fetch the liquid flavouring for the meats or sweets
She was a saucy young woman
 – She was cheeky and made cheeky remarks to young men
That young woman has a sauce
 – She is disrespectful and takes unwarranted liberties

Screw(s)

I am in need of some screws
 – I want some metal fixers to screw into wood
I am in need of a screw
 – I have a strong urge in my trousers

Screwed

He was screwed by his partners
 – He was cheated by them
She was screwed by his partners
 – The vile chaps took turns to have sex with her

"I AM IN NEED OF A SCREW..."

Scrubber
Have you got a floor scrubber?
– I need a brush to clear the floor
Have you got a scrubber on the floor?
– Are you engaged in illicit sexual activity with a less than clean young woman? Getting splinters in her bum?

Seedy
He looked rather seedy
– He didn't look very well
or He looked suspicious, shabby and shambling

Sensible/sensuous
She was very sensible
– She was of good behaviour and good, realistic ideas
She was very sensuous
– She was a hot sexy creature

Served
The waitress served our table
– The lady delivered the meal we had ordered
The rabbit served his doe
– He did what came naturally and rapidly to rabbits

Shagged
I feel shagged
– I am completely tired out
I have been shagged
– A nasty man has just taken sexual advantage of me

Sheath
He put a sheath on his weapon
– He put his sword in its scabbard
He put his weapon in a sheath
– He encased his whatsit in a rubber contraceptive

Shelf
His daughter is at the shelf
– She is fetching something from the shelf
His daughter is on the shelf
– She is unmarried and likely to remain so

Short
He has fat hairy short arms
  – His arms are hairy and short
He has a fat hairy short arm
  – His male appendage is as described
He was caught short of cash
  – He did not have enough money
He was caught short
  – He was so in need of bowel evacuation that he was desperate

Short and curly
I would like to run my fingers through your short and curly hair
  – I want to stroke your bubble-cut head
I would like to run my fingers through your short and curlies
  – I am a low person wishing to play with your private parts

Slag
Slag is the normally difficult to use or sell residue of coal mining
A slag is a worn out, too willing, not very attractive female

Slash
The football hooligans slashed the carriage seats
  – They cut the cushion with razors
They slashed out of the train window
  – They risked agonising electrocution by urinating out of the window

Smut
She had smut on her nose
  – She had specks of dirt on her nose
She was very smutty
  – She told dirty jokes or used rude language

Sod
He turned the sod
  – He dug the earth
He turned, the sod
  – The low down chap turned round

Spanking
I have a spanking new girlfriend

– I have a completely new lady friend

I have a new spanking girlfriend

– I have a female friend who enjoys mild flagellation

Spitting

She was the spitting image of her sister

– She looked exactly like her sister

She was spitting at the image of her sister

– This female was expectorating at the photograph of her sister

Spoof

I went to a spoof dinner party

– I went to a pretence dinner party that made fun of the subject of dining

I went to a poof's dinner party

– This queer was giving it

Spotted dick

I've spotted Dick

– I have just caught sight of Richard

I'd like some spotted dick

– May I have some of that steamed pudding with raisins in it?

He has got a spotted dick

– He should consult a venereologist

Spout

He loves to stand and spout

– He likes rambling on verbally about this and that

That engine is up the spout

– The motor is not working properly

He put her up the spout

– He made her pregnant

Spud

He was walking round eating a big spud

– Eating a large potato

He was walking round with a big spud

– He had a great hole in the heel of his sock

Spunk
He has lots of spunk
– *either* He is extremely brave
or His sexual emissions are extremely voluminous

Stacked
He is well stacked
– He has lots and lots and lots of money
She is well stacked
– She has big tits

Stew
He ate stew
– He ate boiled or simmered meats
He was in a stew
– He was agitated and didn't know what to do
or He was in a low down brothel

Sticky
My palm feels sticky
– It is hot here and the inside of my hand is hot and sweaty
He has a sticky palm
– He steals or takes bribes

Stimulate
His conversation stimulated her
– The brilliance of his verbal ability got her mind in a whirl
He stimulated her
– His low down gropings got something else in a whirl

Stool
The milkmaid sat on her stool
– She sat on a three legged chair
The milkmaids sat on their stools
– They sat on their solid waste matter

Stuff
She is often stuffy
– She is frequently pompous
She is partial to stuffing
– *either* She likes things like sage and onion with her meat
or She enjoys sex

Suggestion
He was full of suggestions
– He gave lots of ideas
He was very suggestive
– He gave sexy hints all the time

Supposition/suppository
Let us take a supposition and work it out from that
– Start with an assumption of what might have been
Take a suppository
– A solid, bullet shaped ointment used for anal insertion

Swing
My wife adores swing
– She likes music with a hot beat
My wife adores swinging
– She likes husband swapping

Tail
He was tailing the beans
– He was chopping the ends off
He was tailing her
– He was a detective following her
He gave her tail
– He performed on her

Tap
He tapped him
– He gave him a gentle knock
He is at the tap
– He is getting some water
He is on the tap
– He is trying to borrow money

Tart
I love sticking my teeth into a tasty tart
– *either* I enjoy a filled sweet pastry
or I enjoy a willing young lady

Tease
She was teasing her boyfriend
– She was making jokes with him
She is a tease
– She excites men but never delivers the goodies

That
I would like a bit of that
– *either* I am pointing to what I would enjoy
or I am in need of sexual gratification

Tinkle
Could you give me a tinkle?
– Please phone me about it
I am going for a tinkle
– I am going to the urinal to pass water

Titbit
He looked for a tasty titbit
– He searched for a nice edible morsel
He looked for a tasty bit of tit
– He searched for a good looking young female

Tits
Look at those two tits in the garden
– There are two little birds in the garden
Just look at those tits over there
– A girl with large bosoms is over there
(See also **Boobs**)

Tools
The plumber put his tools away and left the bathroom
– The man mending pipes replaced his spanners and left
The plumber put his tool away
– He did his trousers up properly so no pipes hung out

Tossed

He tossed himself off the pier

- The poor man tried to commit suicide by throwing himself out to sea

He tossed himself off at the pier

- The dirty chap masturbated at the seaside

Touch up

The artist touched up the painting of his model

- He added a few brush lines here and there

The artist touched up his model

- He tickled her with his brush on her private parts

Tramp

He is a tramp

- He is a hobo traveller and scruffy and smelly

She is a tramp

- She consorts with anything that moves in trousers

Tricks

A conjurer knows a lot of tricks

- He has a large repertoire of illusions

My girlfriend knows a lot of tricks

- She has a large repertoire of skills gleaned from the Kama Sutra and The Joy of Sex

Trot

He is coping very well with the trot

- He is on a horse and controlling it while it is trotting

He is coping very well with the trots

- He is controlling his frequent loose bowel movements

Vetted

I have been vetted

- My bona fides have been thoroughly checked

My dog has been vetted

- His sex life has been permanently checked

Vice

The vice was kept in the workshop

- The metal clamp was placed there

The workshop was the vice centre
– Illegal naughty things went on there
Solitary vice went on in the workshop
– Masturbation went on there

Walker
She is a shop walker
– She is a roving senior supervisor in a shop
She is a keen road walker
– She belongs to a club that goes on long distance walks
She is a keen street walker
– She is an enthusiastic prostitute

Wall
He has driven me to the wall
– He has made me bankrupt
He has driven me up the wall
– He has made me nearly crazy

Well hung
That game looks well hung
– Those wild birds have been allowed to rot for the appropriate time
The men playing that game look well hung
– The players appear to have large appendages

Welsh
He liked the Welsh
– He enjoyed the company of people from Wales
He liked to welsh
– He was fond of failing to meet his obligations

Wick
She lowered the wick on the heater
– She lowered the absorbent burning part
He showed her his wick
– He was a flasher

Whip
He whipped a horse today
– *either* He hit the poor creature with a leather thong

or He stole a horse today

Wind

He's got wind of it
 – He has heard of the secret
He's got wind
 – He is flatulent or bloated

Windbreak

I am looking for the windbreak place
 – I need to hire a canvas structure that prevents the cold wind reaching me
I am looking for a place to break wind
 – I wish to fart away from you lot

Winkle

He was picking at a winkle
 – He had a pin to remove the edible part of a small mollusc
He was picking at his winkle
 – The dirty chap was playing with his privates
The troops winkled out the enemy
 – They picked them one by one out of their hideyholes
The troops took their winkles out at the enemy
 – They undid their garments and waved their fleshy weapons at the enemy

Part three

Some confusing definitions

A list showing that every word you say could cause you problems. These are not the only meanings of the words but they should serve to cause reasonable confusion.

An abandoned child – one who has been deserted
An abandoned woman – one who has become immoral
A board – a piece of wood
A bawd – a professionally promiscuous female
Abroad – overseas
A broad – a likely female
Affected – caused change
Affected – put on and snobby
Advances – made by banks or money lenders
Advances – made by young men towards females they fancy
Affairs – smart social functions
Affairs – sexual liaisons
A lien – a legal hold on property
Alien – foreign
Aloofer – being rather more stuck up and self important
A loofah – what you use to wash your back in the bath
A moor – a man from part of Spain
Amour – love in any language
Annal – a history
Anal – relates to your nether channel
Ape – a monkey
Ape – to copy
A rest – a pause perhaps for relaxation
Arrest – being detained by the law
Assert – to state positively

A cert – a girl sure to deliver the goods
Assist – to give help
A cyst – sometimes painful nodule
A stern look – disapproving
Astern – to the rear of somebody or something
Attack – an assault
A tack – A small nail or a guiding stitch
Attempting – trying
A tract – a heavy literary work
Averse – being against
A verse – a bit of a poem

Back side – part of a bacon joint
Backside – your posterior
Badger – a mammal
Badger – to pester and annoy
Baffle – a device for preventing excess noise
Baffle – to mystify
Bag – a handy carrier
Bag – to kill or capture birds or animals
Bag – a rude description of a coarse female
Baggage – suitcases and personal effects
Baggage – a flighty unreliable female
Bale – a secured package
Bail – what is demanded as surety to release a prisoner
Bald – hairless
Bawled – making a lot of noise
Ball – a grand dance
Ball – a spherical object
Ball – a testicle
Balmy – refers to a calm pleasantly warm day
Barmy – daft and mentally unsound
Bandy – to exchange words to and fro
Bandy – bow legged
Bar – to prevent
Bar – where you booze
Bar – a bit of wood or iron
Bare faced – clean shaven or with smooth cheeks
Barefaced – unashamed effrontery
Barely – scarcely

Barely – in the nude
Barmy – see Balmy
Barracks – where troops are kept
Barrack – to jeer
Barren – empty
Baron – a titled gent
Baron – a lump of meat
Base – a home centre
Base – bottom
Batman – hangs around with Robin
Batman – guides planes with his bats after landing
Batman – a servant for an officer
Battery – powers a torch
Battery – a military unit
Battery – goes with assault when people get hit
Beard – a hairy chin
Beard – to grab in order to speak with
Bearish – rude behaviour
Barish – rather undressed or bare
Beau – a gallant boy friend or fop
Bow – a curly twirly tie or lace
Beef – the flesh of the cow or bull
Beef – to complain constantly
Beer – what you drink
Bier – what you are carried out on when you are dead
Beet – a plant
Beat – hit
Beat – an erection
Belt – what holds up your trousers
Belt – to hit
Berth – a place on a ship
Birth – what happens when you are born
Bilge – the inner base part of a ship
Bilge – rubbish
Bill – the outstanding beak of a bird
Bill – the outstanding amount due to be paid
Bit – goes in a horse's mouth
Bit – a small piece
Bit – a friendly female piece
Blast – the effect of an explosion
Blast – an expletive or a telling off

Bloomers – flowers that are fully open
Bloomers – loaves of bread
Bloomers – long old fashioned ladies' knickers
Bore – to drill a hole
Bore – to tire out by being uninteresting
Boar – a male pig
Boot – footwear with ankle cover
Boot – an over willing female
Bootie – small baby's footwear
Booty – what a thief gathers
Boy – young male
Buoy – floating thing boats avoid or tie up to
Brain – what controls your thinking
Brain – to bash on the head
Brake – to slow down or what slows you down
Break – to shatter or smash
Brass – an alloy of copper; money
Brass – a prostitute
Brawn – the result of boiling a pig's head
Brawn – lots of muscle
Bridle – straps round the head of a horse
Bridle – reject in anger
Bridal – relating to a bride
Briefs – what barristers have as instructions
Briefs – ladies' and gents' underwear
Bucket shop – where pails are sold
Bucket shop – where dubious shares are sold
Buck – male animal
Buck – to fight against the system
Bull – male cow
Bull – military excess of spit and polish
Bull – load of verbal rubbish
Butt – the shouldering part of a rifle
Butt – to assault with the head foremost
Butt – a large liquid measure
Butt – your backside
Buyer – someone who buys
Byre – a shed where cows are kept

Caddie – man who carries golf clubs for others
Caddy – container for tea

Calving – act of giving birth to a calf
Carving – slice up as in meat
Camp – collection of tents
Camp – high fashion or homosexual
Candid – direct, straightforward
Candied – covered in sugar as a preservative
Cannon – large gun
Cannon – rebound off another object
Canon – a cathedral clergyman
Caper – pickled nasturtium seed
Caper – a jaunt without serious purpose
Caper – to leap about
Cap size – size of flat headwear
Capsize – to overturn
Carp – common freshwater fish
Carp – keep complaining
Cashier – dismissal with dishonour of an army officer
Cashier – person who disburses and receives cash
Cast – what comes out of a sculpting mould
Cast – characters in a play
Cast – thrown afar
Cast – sort of squint in an eye
Caste – Indian social class
Ceiling – top of a room
Sealing – hunting seals
Sealing – sticking down tightly
Chap – to crack from the cold (skin)
Chap – a man loosely described
Char – to burn, usually on the outside
Char – an office or house cleaner
Char – a cup of tea
Charge – to rush at
Charge – require payment
Charge – to accuse
Charge – to impose a duty upon
Chased – rushed after
Chaste – unspoiled, virginal
Cheap – inexpensive
Cheep – the sound of a bird
Choky – causing choking
Choky – prison

Chuck – to throw
Chuck – to tickle (as under the chin)
Chuck – the holding part of a machine tool
Chute – a slope or tunnel
Shoot – to fire
Clap – applaud by striking hands together
Clap – gonorrhoea
Clock – a machine for recording the time
Clock – to hit hard
Clog – to cram up or prevent movement by jamming
Clog – wooden shoe
Club – an association of people
Club – a wooden or metal offensive weapon
Club – a golf stick
Coarse – rough in texture
Coarse – rude and offensive
Course – a set system of study
Course – channel of a river or canal
Cod – large fleshy fish
Cod – a male sex organ
Cod – to fool
Common – ordinary, rather vulgar
Common – available for everybody
Common – open land in public ownership
Conquer – to vanquish, overcome
Conker – horse chestnut used for children's games
Continent – the large mainland
Continent – able to control bowel functions or carnal desires
Copse – small wooded patch
Cops – police
Corporation – municipal or business body usually large
Corporation – belly
Coupling – link in a chain
Coupling – having sex relations
Crackers – crisp biscuits
Crackers – paper novelty containers
Crackers – crazy
Crib – a baby's cot
Crib – to prevent action by cramping
Crib – to cheat by copying the work of others
Curb – to restrain

Kerb – the side of the pavement
Cut – slit, carve, shorten
Cut – drunk

Dab – press softly, as on a wound
Dab – small flat fish
Dab – clever at
Dam – animal mother
Dam – water barrier or raiser
Damn – a mild expletive, to condemn
Dear – expensive
Dear – term of endearment
Deer – an animal
Die – to finish life
Die – metal stamping device
Dye – to soak in colours
Dike – ditch, wall or hillock built to hold back or retain water
Dike – a lesbian
Dish – container, usually for food
Dish – course of a meal
Dish – pretty girl
Dish – to prevent or frustrate
Dock – to cut or shorten
Dock – a harbour for ships
Dock – where the prisoner stands in court
Dock – plant used as antidote to stinging nettles
Doe – female deer
Dough – from which bread is made
Dough – cash
Dual – serving two purposes, a pair
Duel – contest between two people, sometimes fatal

Effected – caused changes
Affected – put on, snobby
Egg – what chickens lay
Egg – to nag, to spur on
Emit – to let out, to issue
A mit – a hand
Enact – to cause a law to be completed

An act – a part of a play
Erection – something being built, the act of building
Erection – a penis fully extended
Exact – precise
Exact – levy money or a tax from

Fabricate – to build
Fabricate – to make up a lie
Fag – tiring task
Fag – cigarette
Fag – homosexual
Fag – servant to another boy at public school
Faggot – sort of slab of minced meat
Faggot – twig bundle for fire
Faggot – homosexual
Fair – just and honourable
Fair – blonde, light
Fair – market or peripatetic entertainment
Fairy – a mythical sprite
Fairy – homosexual
Fan – device for causing a blow of air
Fan – fervent supporter
Fan – a female's whatsit
Farther – a longer distance
Father – male parent
Father – act of procreation by a male
Fawn – to praise and honour hypocritically
Fawn – sort of brown colour
Fawn – offspring of a deer
Faint – barely perceptible
Faint – a momentary collapse
Fertiliser – one who spreads manure
Fertiliser – manure good for plants
Fertiliser – one who passes male seed
Fetching – act of bringing
Fetching – attractive
Few – just a small number
Phew – an expletive expressing heat or the smell in a room
Fiddler – violinist
Fiddler – a cheat

Fine – excellent
Fine – thin and delicate
Fine – a cash penalty imposed on an offender
Fire – burning collection of material
Fire – to sack, dispense with the services
Fishy – similar to a fish
Fishy – strange or illegal events
Flap – to lose control quickly
Flap – a ledge
Flap – to wave up and down
Flea – small biting insect
Flee – to run away to safety
Fleece – sheep's woollen coat
Fleece – to rob or strip all possessions
Flog – hit or strike with a weapon
Flog – to sell
Flower – a blossom
Flour – ground wheat or maize
Flu – influenza
Flu – human base orifice
Flue – chimney outlet for smoke
Flew – progressed through the air
Fluke – parasite, usually in the liver
Fluke – lucky chance
Flush – full of money
Flush – to release down the toilet with water
Flush – to redden
Fly – small insect
Fly – very sharp witted (derogatory)
Fly – see Flew
Fool – an idiot, figure of fun
Fool – kind of soft dessert
Frank – to stamp with a duty paid sign
Frank – direct, honest, sincere
Fray – battle or fight
Fray – rub away at the edges
Friar – type of monk
Fryer – one who fries
Fudge – sort of soft toffee
Fudge – cover up and confuse

Gall – bitter substance relating to the gall bladder
Gall – outrageous effrontery
Game – sport, contest, pastime
Game – partridges, pheasants, wild birds
Game – (fair game) a person ready to be taken
Gas – airborne substances, vapours
Gas – constant talking
Gay – happy, uninhibited
Gay – homosexual
Goalie – goalkeeper
Goolie – testicle
Grafter – one who grafts shoots on trees or plants
Grafter – hard worker
Grafter – a swindler through bribery
Grass – green herbaceous plant
Grass – to tell on your friends, to give away secrets
Grass – marijuana
Grease – to apply lubricant
Grease – oily fatty substance
Grease – to bribe
Grind – to fine down by abrasion
Grind – hard work
Grind – the sex act
Gross – before deductions
Gross – 144
Gross – fat, ungainly, coarse
Group – number with direct relationships
Group – collection of people with common purpose
Groupie – girl who hangs around pop groups distributing sexual favours to them all

Hack – to cut indiscriminately
Hack – an all purpose horse
Hack – low grade writer
Ham – type of smoked or cured pork
Ham – an overacting actor
Hash – mixture of meats or meat and vegetables
Hash – a disorganised effort, a mess
Hash – marijuana
High – tall, lofty

High – malodorous
High – drunk
Homely – domesticated, a warm friendly residence
Homely – plain or ugly
Hood – a cloth or material covering
Hood – front top of a car
Hood – a petty gangster
Hop – a plant from which beer is made
Hop – to jump or move forward on one leg
Hop – common low down dance
Horny – being covered by bony hard or scaly substances
Horny – having an erection
Hump – a disfigured spine
Hump – brow of a hill
Hump – annoyance
Hump – the sex act

Importune – to beg or seek assistance from another
Importune – to approach for an immoral purpose
Impotent – without power, unable to assist
Impotent – lacking the sexual necessary
Insist – demand, press
Incest – sex relations with close relatives
In sight – can be seen
Incite – to urge towards a course of action
Intercourse – social or verbal relationship
Intercourse – sex between persons
Interfere – to meddle
Interfere with – to assault sexually
Intern – incarcerate
Intern – hospital resident senior student
In turn – one at a time

Jack – a man's name
Jack – a device for holding or lifting things
Jack – the Knave in a pack of cards
Jack – on his own
Jack – the sex act
Jade – semi precious stone

Jade – unfaithful woman
Jar – glass or pottery container
Jar – sudden physical shock
Jerk – to pull suddenly or unevenly
Jerk – term of opprobrium for a man without scruples
Junket – milk or cream curdled, with rennet
Junket – an uninhibited party

Kerb – the side of a pavement
Curb – to restrain
Kinky – having a small twist in it – as in a rope
Kinky – desirous of unusual sex practices
Knacker – someone whose job is slaughtering horses for their hoofs and hide
Knackers – testicles
Knackered – tired out
Knockers – people who knock
Knockers – metal hinged objects on doors
Knockers – female breasts
Knit – to join together
Nit – small insect
Nit – an idiot

Lag – to cover or protect
Lag – to dawdle, stay behind others
Lag – an habitual jailbird
Lapse – period of time
Lapse – an omission of duty
Laps – the tops of people's knees when sitting
Lark – small songbird
Lark – a prank, a practical joke, a pleasing pastime
Lay – unordained or unqualified
Lay type of song
Lay – the act of ovulation
Lay – a female candidate for sex
Leek – type of onion
Leak – outflow of liquid or information
Leak – urinate
Lick – to stroke with the tongue

Lick – to beat in a fight
Lights – lamps, illuminations
Lights – lungs of some animals
Loaf – shape of bread
Loaf – to laze about
Lovely child – a beautiful child
Love child – a bastard
Lusty – loud, strong, full of effort
Lusty – full of lust, lascivious

Madam – polite form of address for ladies
Madam – reference to a haughty spoilt, petulent female who always wants her own way
Madam – controller of a brothel
Maidenhood – the time spent as a young unmarried woman
Maidenhead – a woman's hymen, virginity
Mate – a friend
Mate – referring to animals procreating
Mealy – corn meal, ground maize
Mealy mouthed – a term of opprobrium suggesting an unworthy unctuous manner
Medals – tokens and decorations for valour or worthy military service
Medals – fly buttons
Mince – meat chopped very small
Mince – walking with a hurried wobbly gait, like a stage queer
Mistress – female head of the house
Mistress – a school teacher
Mistress – a man's extra marital partner
Mockers – those who mock or deride
Mockers – 'Put the mockers on' – to make unlucky
Monkeys – hairy mammals
Monkeys – 'Don't give a monkeys' – shortened phrase relating to a monkey's sex habits
Monthlies – magazines that appear once a month
Monthlies – menstruation
Motion – a change in position, mobility
Motion – a resolution at a meeting
Motion – solid faecal movement
Mug – solid drinking vessel

Mug – a fool who is easily fooled
Mug – to study, e.g. for an examination
Mug – to hit and rob
Mummy – a colloquial way of saying mother
Mummy – a wrapped preserved corpse, embalmed
Muscle – body tissue
Mussel – small mollusc

Nephrites – types of stone of which jade is a variety
Nephritis – kidney disease
Nibble – to eat in small bites
Nibble – to engage in sexual dalliance
Nick – to cut slightly, to carve a segment
Nick – to steal
Nip – to move fast
Nip – to pinch with the fingers
Nip – a Japanese
Nob – smart person
Nob – the head
Knob – the penis
Nob – a handle (knob)
None – not one, not any
Nun – a chaste female, member of a religious order
Nut – metal fixer with a thread
Nut – the seed kernal of certain fruits
Nut – slang for head
Nut – a lunatic

Organ – large musical instrument
Organ – a functional part of the body
Organ – colloquially one's pudendal parts

Pain – suffering, anguish, a sharp ache
Pane – piece of window glass
Peer – member of the aristocracy
Peer – to glance searchingly
Pee-er – one who urinates
Pervert – to distort or change the course to the bad

Pervert – a kink, a person with a liking for unnatural acts
Penal – oppressive, related to the prison system
Penile – relating to a penis
Pet – small domesticated animal kept for friendship
Pet – to pet is to have mild sexual touching or stroking
Phlegm – to have phlegm may be to denote a cool stolid manner
Phlegm – to have phlegm may refer to an excess of mucal secretion
Pike – a fighting fish
Piker – a cheat
Piles – mounds, untidy heaps
Piles – large wooden or concrete main supports
Piles – haemorrhoids
Poke – to prod
Poke – a sort of purse
Poke – to have sex with (m-f)
Poop – the rear upper part of a ship
Poop – slang word for excreta
Porridge – oatmeal breakfast food
Porridge – slang word for jail sentence
Posterior – rear part of anything
Posterior – rear private parts, backside
Prick – to prod with a pointed instrument. To thin out (in plants)
Prick – male sex organ
Privates – a collection of soldiers of the basic rank
Privates – sex organs
Privy – secret, privileged
Privy – lavatory

Quad – four sided
Quod – prison
Queen – female royalty
Queen – elderly homosexual
Queer – strange, unusual
Queer – homosexual

Racket – unseemly noise
Racket – a bat for playing tennis
Racket – somewhat illegal scheme for raising money
Ram – male sheep

Ram – to barge into
Ram – sexually profligate male
Rank – straight row of men
Rank – degree or order in society of a person
Rank – malodorous and stale
Raspberry – fruit
Raspberry – rude noise
Rectal – relating to the backside
Rectoral – relating to a Rector in a church or university
Refuse – to deny permission
Refuse – disposable rubbish
Rib – bones of the chest
Rib – to tease
Rut – mark or shallow trench made by a wheel
Rut – to have sex

Scum – greasy, mucky residue
Scum – greasy, mucky, low down people
Seduce – take from the proper path
Seduce – take sexually for the first time from the proper path
Sewer – one who sews
Sewer – the outflow underground for excreta and rainwater
Shag – light tobacco
Shag – to have sex
Sire – an old form of address to a superior
Sire – to father
Sod – earth, soil
Sod – a homosexual
Sow – a female pig
Sow – to scatter seed for planting
Sponger – one who sponges a suit
Sponger – one always on the scrounge
Squirt – to emit a jet of liquid
Squirt – an undersized person
Stimulate – to bring about thoughts, inspire
Stimulate – to bring on sexually
Strip – a narrow piece of land or cloth
Strip – undress
Stud – a bone or metal collar or cloth connector
Stud – a place for procreation of animals

Stud – a male sexually very active

Tapping – drawing liquid from
Tapping – hitting or knocking gently
Tapping – borrowing money
Tart – small filled pastry
Tart – sharp, acidy
Tart – a prostitute or promiscuous woman
Thick – solid, wide dimension
Thick – stupid
Tit – a small bird
Tit – breast
Tool – an implement
Tool – his implement
Twit – to tease
Twit – an idiot

Undone – not done up
Undone – ruined

Venerable – an object of worship or awe
Venereal – relating to venereal disease
Vice – a clamp-like object for gripping things
Vice – undesirable malefactions

Whatnot – an old item of furniture
Whatnot – a personal item of furniture
Wirepuller – one who organises things and people
Wirepuller – a masturbator